Nature's Children

SQUIDS

James Kinchen

FACTS IN BRIEF

Classification of Squids
    Phylum: *Mollusca* (mollusks)
    Class: *Cephalopoda* (cephalopods)
    Order: *Teuthoidea* (squids)
    Species: There are 500 species of squids.

World distribution. All the world's major seas and oceans.

Habitat. Found in all ocean habitats and at all depths. More common in cooler waters.

Distinctive physical characteristics. Streamlined, bullet-shaped bodies; eight sucker-lined arms and two long feeding tentacles; large, well-developed eyes; capable of rapid color changes; many species produce light; parrot-like beak.

Habits. Adults live alone or in large schools. Swim by jet propulsion. Prey is captured with the tentacles. Eggs laid together in large masses. Young float in the plankton until they are able to swim actively. Most adults die soon after spawning.

Diet. Mainly fish, shrimps, and other squids.

All rights reserved. Except for use in a review, no part of this book may be reproduced, stored in a retrieval system, or transmitted in any form, or by any means, electronic, mechanical photocopying, recording, or otherwise, without prior permission of the publisher.

© 1999 Brown Partworks Limited
Printed and bound in U.S.A.
Editor: James Kinchen
Designer: Tim Brown

Published by:

GROLIER EDUCATIONAL

Sherman Turnpike, Danbury, Connecticut 06816

Library of Congress Cataloging-in-Publishing Data
    Squids.
        p. cm. -- (Nature's children. Set 6)
    ISBN 0-7172-9367-X (alk. paper) -- ISBN 0-7172-9351-3 (set)
    1. Squids.--Juvenile Literature. [1. Squids.] I. Grolier Educational (Firm) II. Series.

QL430.2.K56 1999
594'.58—dc21

98-33411

Contents

Back to Front?	Page 6
Mighty Mollusks	Page 9
The Living Fossil	Page 10
Squid Relatives	Page 13
Jet Propelled	Page 14
Arms and Tentacles	Page 17
Hold on Tight!	Page 18
Changing Color	Page 21
Glow in the Dark	Page 22
On the Lookout	Page 25
Smart Creatures	Page 26
Life at the Surface	Page 29
Fierce Hunters	Page 30
Getting Away	Page 33
Deep-Water Dwellers	Page 34
The Kraken	Page 37
Sea-Monster Sightings	Page 38
Giant Squid Facts	Page 39
The Next Generation	Page 42
Living Fast, Dying Young	Page 45
Unknown Animals	Page 46
Words to Know	Page 47
Index	Page 48

A squid patrols the dark surface waters of the Atlantic Ocean.

Imagine standing on the deck of a fishing boat in the middle of the Atlantic Ocean. Gentle waves disturb the silence of the dark night as they lap against the sides of your boat. A movement in the water catches your attention. Darting this way and that, a group of ghostly shapes move in formation across the surface. Lights on their bodies flash in brilliant colors—reds, yellows, and greens. They stare at you with large, intelligent eyes that glow like pale blue lightbulbs. Then they are gone. You might think that you saw aliens, but they were squids.

In all the oceans there are more squids than any other large animal, yet most people have never seen one alive. We are only beginning to understand squids, but already we know that they are among the strangest and most amazing creatures on Earth. Read on to find out more about them.

Back to Front?

If you have ever been in a swimming race, you will know that it is hard work to move quickly through the water. Squids are much faster swimmers than people. Their streamlined bodies are perfect for cutting through the ocean—backward!

The delicate organs that a squid needs to stay alive are kept safe inside a bullet-shaped sac, called the mantle, behind its head. A pair of fins at the tip of the mantle help the squid to steer. At the other end of its body, a squid has eight sucker-lined arms and two long feeding tentacles. These are arranged in a circle around its mouth, which looks like a parrot's beak!

If squids seem totally unlike any of the animals you know, you might be surprised to hear that their relatives are living in the parks and gardens near your home.

A squid has no bones. Instead, its body is supported by a stiff rod, called a pen, inside its mantle.

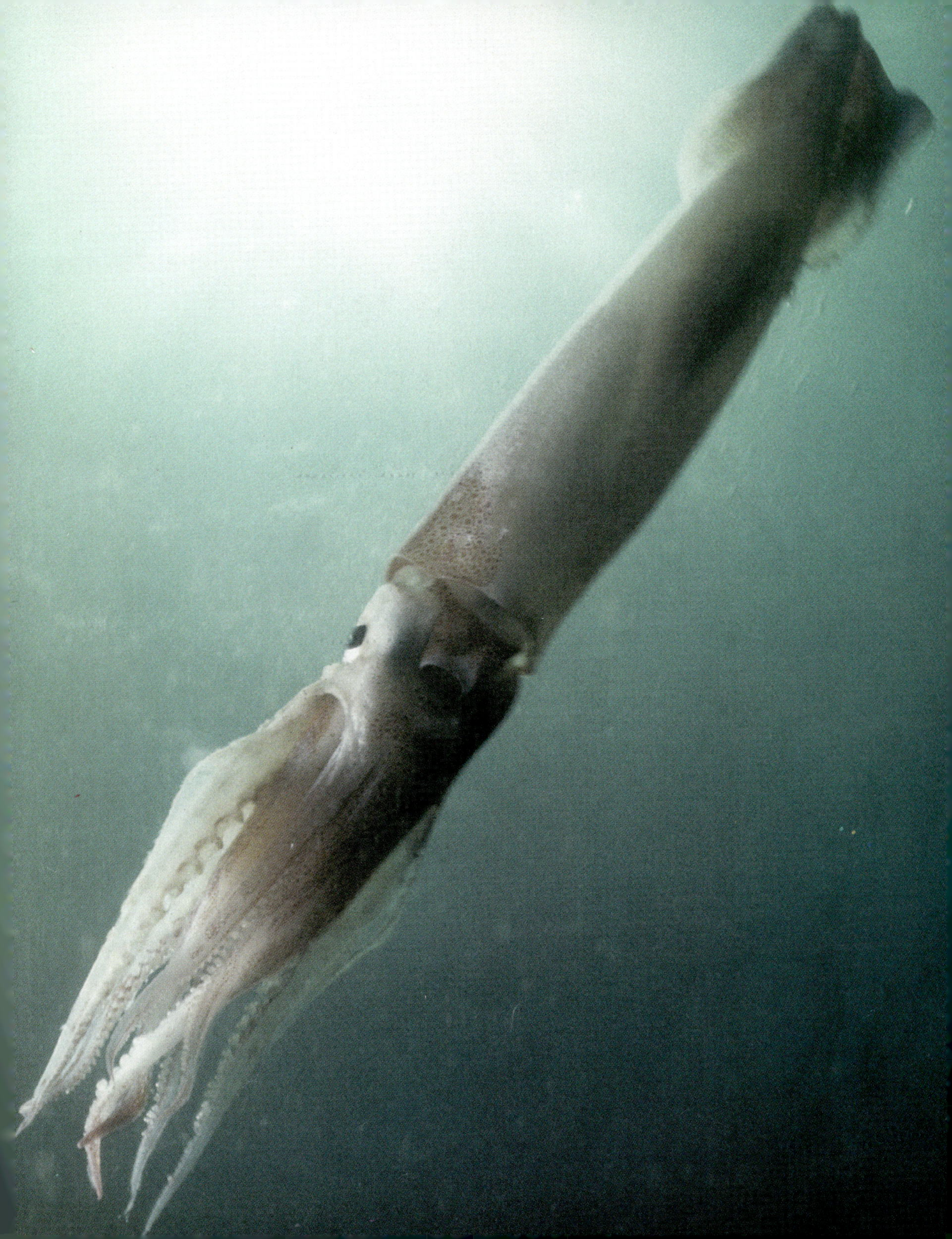

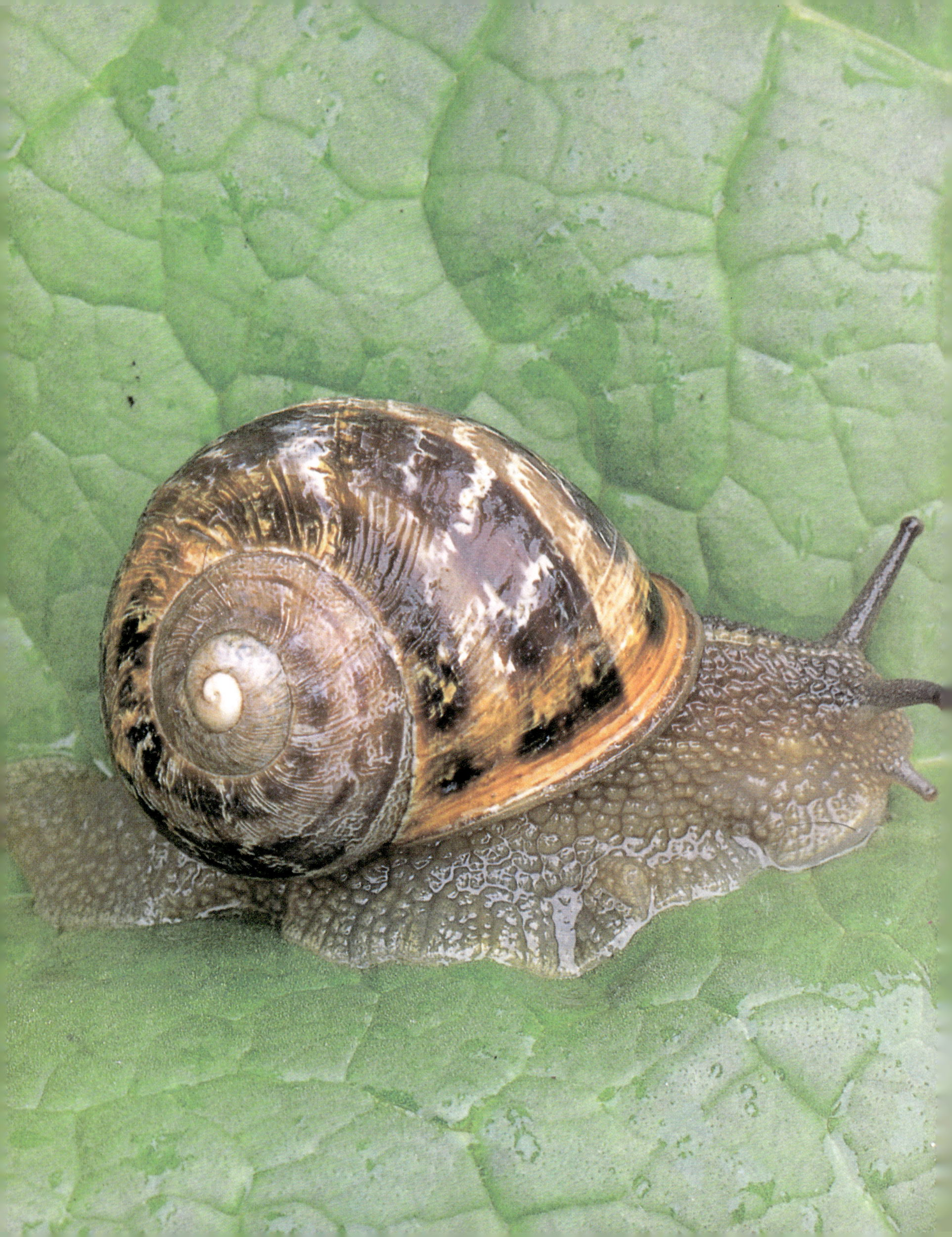

Mighty Mollusks

How is a squid like a snail? At first glance they seem to have very little in common. In fact, they are both part of the same group of animals—the mollusks. There are more than 200,000 different types, or species, of mollusks found all over the world. The snails and slugs in your garden, the limpets and mussels on the seashore, and the squids and octopuses in the oceans are all members of this successful group.

Scientists think that mollusks were the first large animals to swim up away from the bottom of the ocean. Millions of years before the dinosaurs, simple snail-like creatures gave up life on the seabed to float freely in the water. These early swimmers could be the ancestors of modern squids.

Mollusks have soft, fleshy bodies that dry out easily. Slugs and snails are among the few types that can survive on land.

Opposite page:
Unlike a squid, the nautilus has no suckers on its tentacles. Unlike a snail, it lives only in the last section of its shell.

The Living Fossil

Have you ever wondered how we know about the dinosaurs? No one has ever seen one, so all our information comes from studying fossils—the remains of ancient animals preserved in rocks. Scientists thought, from studying fossil shells, that the ancient swimming mollusks had died out millions of years ago. Imagine their surprise when fishermen in the Pacific Ocean said they had seen the creatures, alive!

These secretive animals, called nautiluses, have 38 tentacles around their mouths and shells that look like snail shells. We do not know what they eat, how they catch their food, or why they survived while all of their relatives died out.

Early squids might have looked a bit like nautiluses. As they became faster swimmers, however, their shells got smaller to make their bodies more streamlined. Today the pen inside a squid's body is all that is left of the shell.

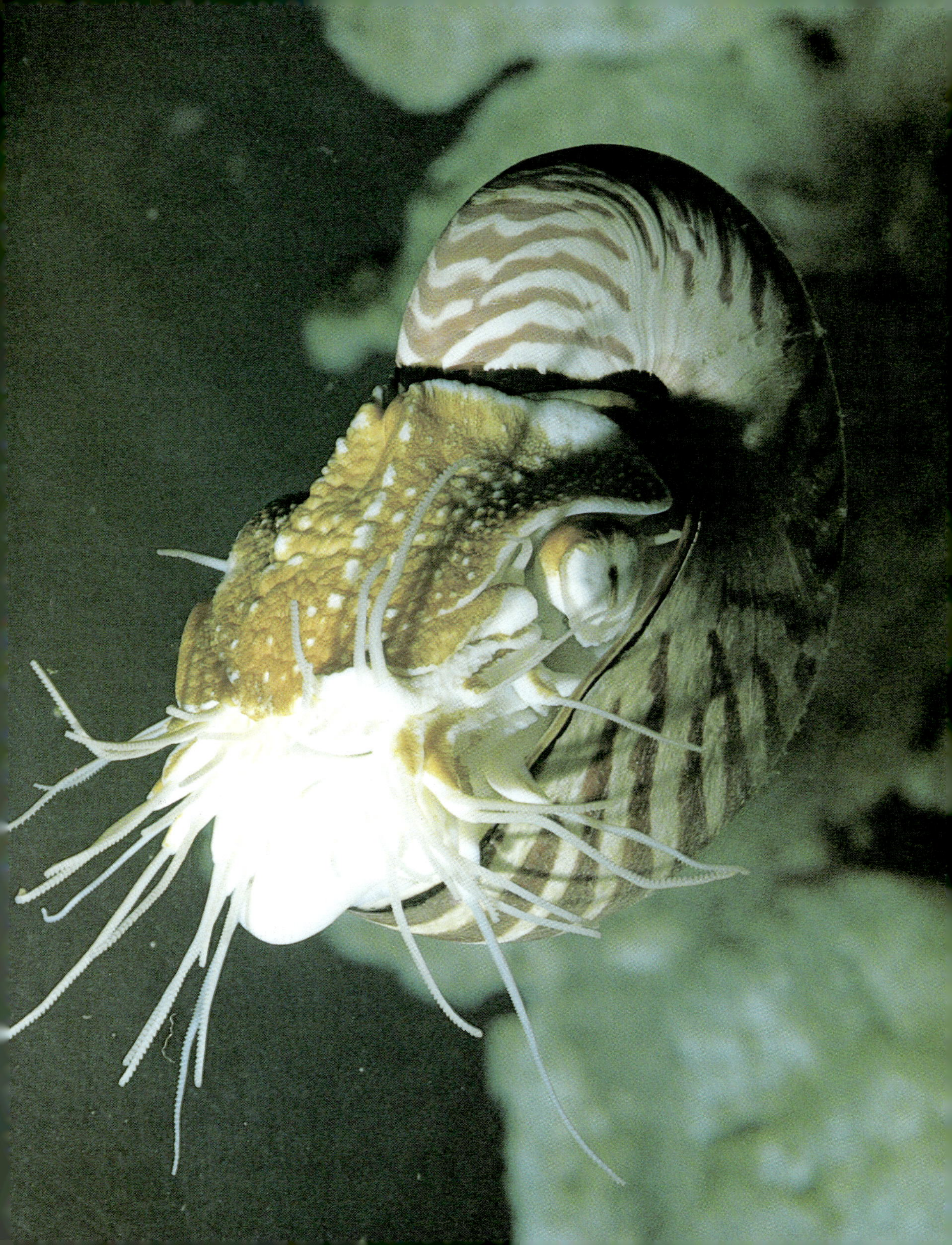

Many cephalopods are poisonous. The blue-ringed octopus from the Pacific only grows to the size of your fist, but its bite can kill a man.

Squid Relatives

Squids, octopuses, and cuttlefish are part of a family of mollusks called cephalopods. You might have seen an octopus in an aquarium. Like squids, they have eight arms, but their bodies are less sleek, and they do not have tentacles. Most types live on or near the seabed where they hunt for crabs and lobsters. Octopuses are weak swimmers and usually walk around on their arms.

Cuttlefish are very similar to squids but have shorter, thicker bodies and are not such fast swimmers. They live close to the shore and ambush passing shrimps and small fish. Cuttlefish pens, called cuttlebones, are often washed up on beaches.

All cephalopods are fierce hunters. Their powerful arms keep a tight grip while they devour their victims, piece by piece, with their sharp beaks.

Jet Propelled

What powers many of our fastest machines? The answer is jet engines. Squids also use jet power. In fact, they have been getting around this way for millions of years.

Squids breathe by sucking water into their mantles then pumping it out of a flexible tube, called the funnel, below their heads. Inside the mantle feathery gills absorb the oxygen in the water. The muscles that do this pumping are much stronger than they need to be just for breathing. A powerful squirt sends the squid shooting off in the opposite direction. Better still, the faster they swim, the more water they pass over their gills, so squids are never out of breath. The fastest squids can zoom along at 20 miles per hour (32 kilometers per hour)—faster than you can run.

Although they prefer to go backward, squids can swim in any direction they choose by moving their flexible funnels.

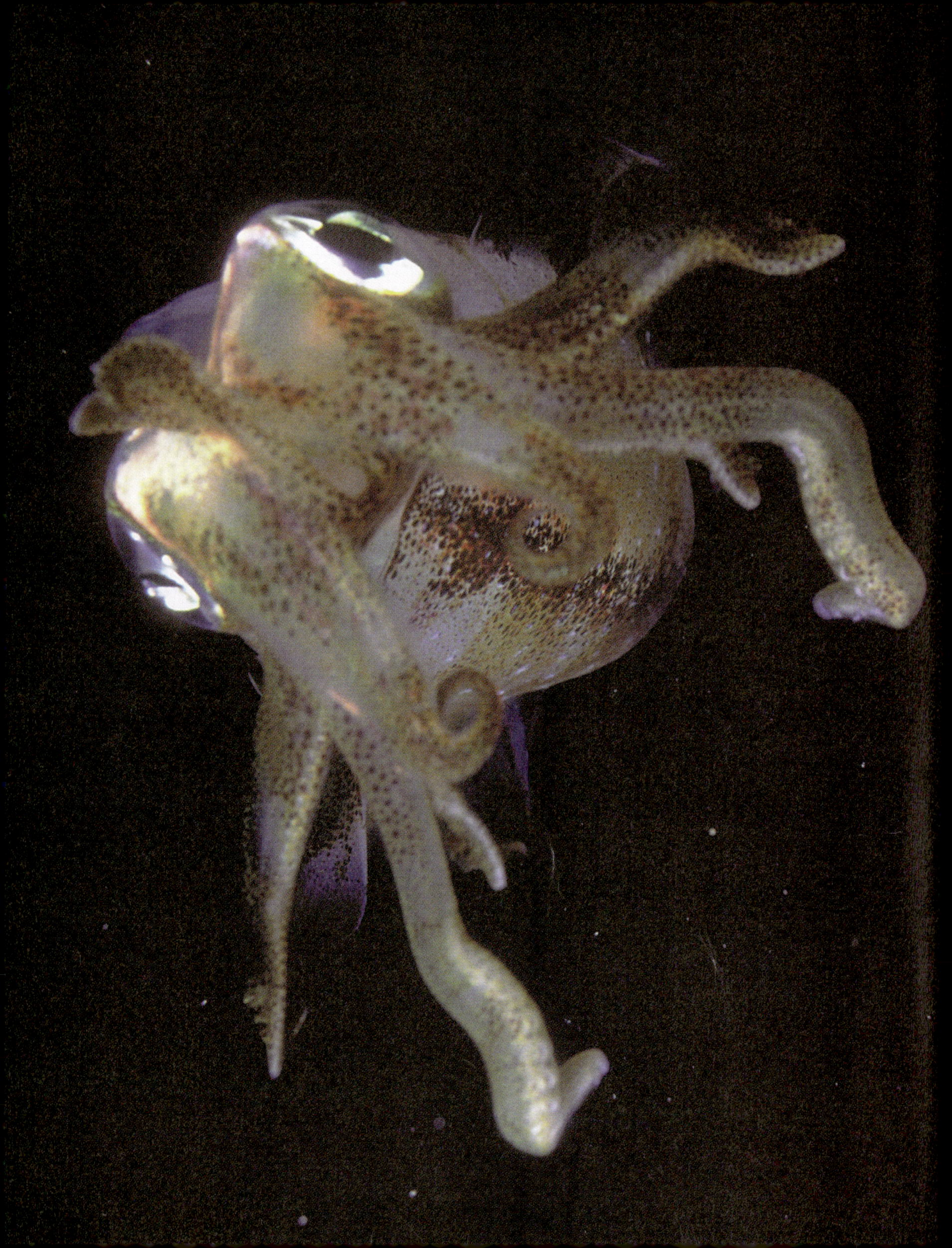

Arms and Tentacles

A squid's prize possessions are the two long feeding tentacles that it keeps safely tucked away in pouches beside its beak. Twice as long as the rest of the squid's body, each tentacle consists of a long, slender stalk with a broad pad at the tip.

When it is hunting, a squid first sneaks up on its prey, edging closer by rippling its fins. Then, like a pair of tongs, the tentacles shoot out and grab the chosen victim. A squid only gets one try at this. If it misses, the prey often escapes while the squid tries to untangle itself.

Try moving your tongue. Like a squid's arms, it contains no bones, but you can curl and twist it to touch any part of your mouth. Imagine having eight tongues! You could use them to hold on to your food, which is how a squid uses its arms. Squids can even taste with their arms to find out if things they catch are good to eat.

A popeye squid prepares to shoot out its long tentacles.

Hold on Tight!

Squids have suckers running the full length of their arms and on the pads of their tentacles. You have probably seen rubber suckers used to stick things to windows or walls, or to clear blocked drains. Squids use their suckers to hold onto their prey—often slippery animals like fish—so each sucker has a row of razor sharp "teeth" around the rim. In some types of squids these teeth grow very large and look similar to a tiger's claws. Fortunately most of their owners live in deep water and rarely come in contact with people!

Squids also use their suckers for defense. Sperm whales, which eat squids, often have rows of circular scars on their heads. These could be marks made by the suckers of monster squids during battles in the depths of the ocean.

Very few animals escape from the deadly suckers of a Humbolt squid.

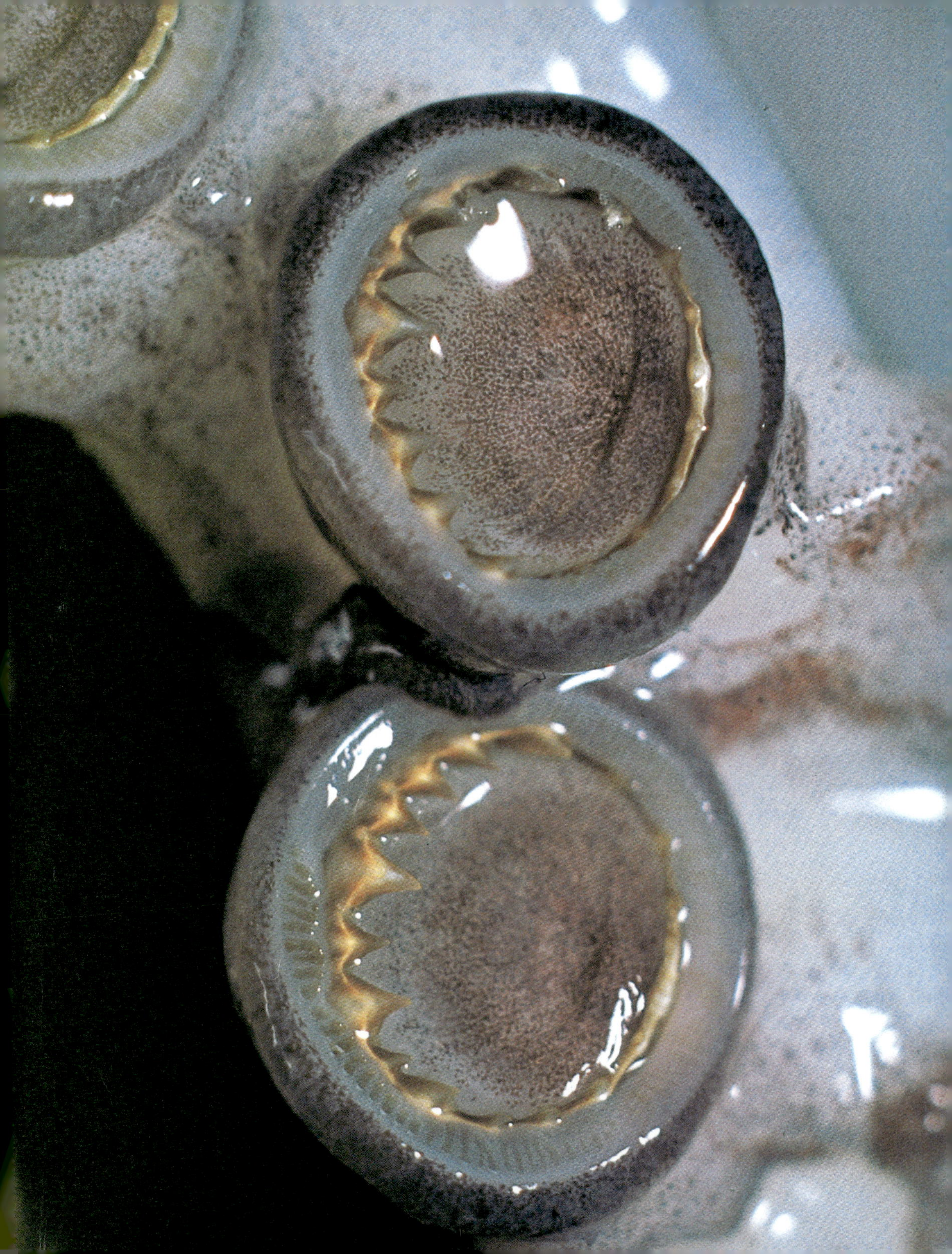

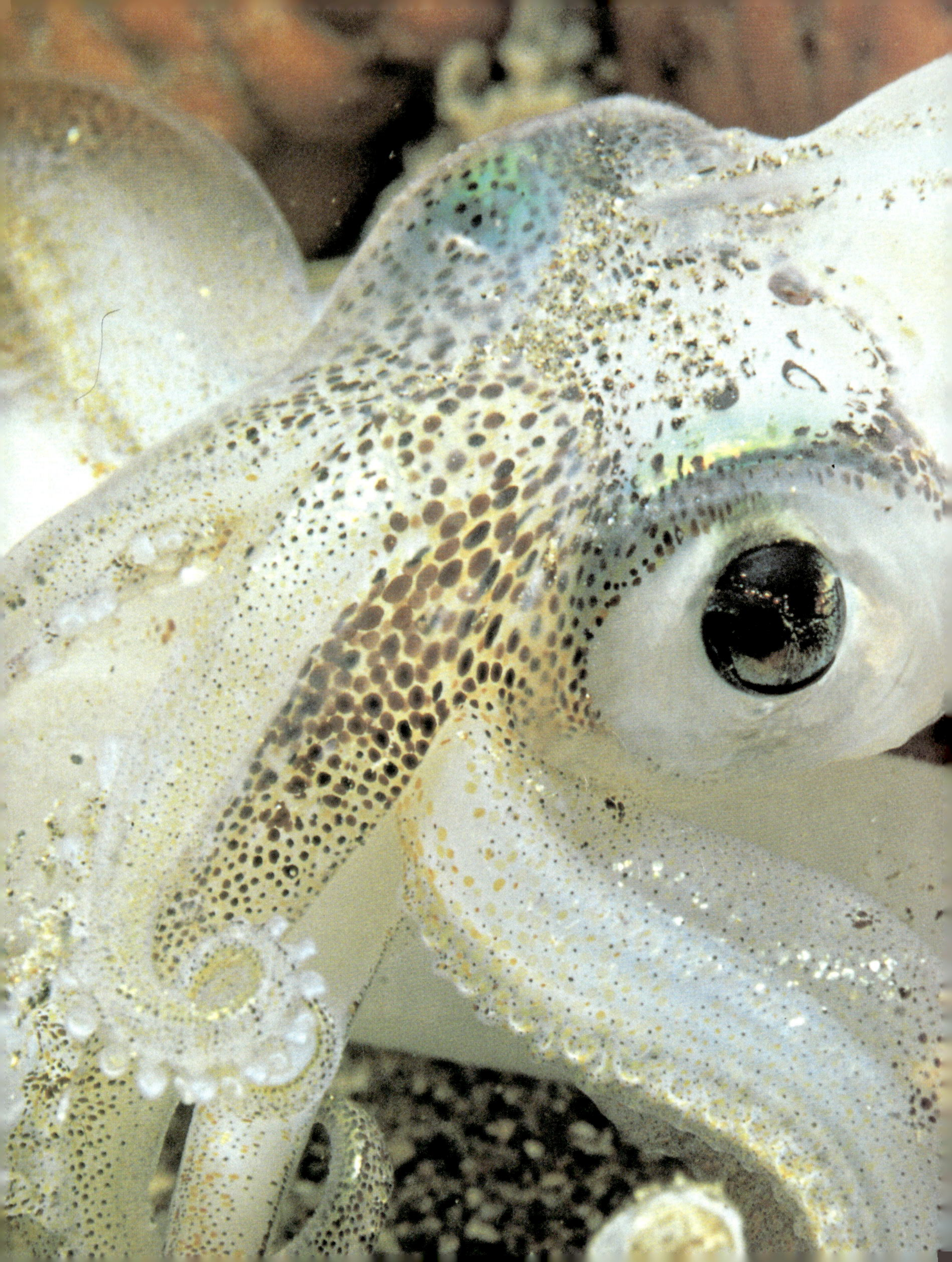

Changing Color

Have you ever wished that you could make yourself invisible? Think of all the tricks you could play. People would not notice you sneaking up on them, and no one would ever be able to find you. Squids are masters of making themselves invisible. Their secret is being able to change color.

A few land animals, such as chameleons, change their color to match their surroundings, but this takes them several minutes. Squids can change color in a fraction of a second. They can even copy complex patterns, like the squares of a checker board.

Squids have little bags of ink, called chromatophores, in their skins. Like tiny lumps of dough, these can be rolled out flat to cover a large area, or squashed up into a tiny ball. If a squid wants to turn red, it just rolls out its red chromatophores until they cover its whole body. The skin itself is see-through, so when a squid wants to vanish, it squeezes all of its colors back into dots.

Opposite page: Squids use color to express their feelings. When excited, they often flash deep red, and groups stay in touch by flashing patterns at one another.

Glow in the Dark

Sunlight does not penetrate very far into the oceans. Deeper than 300 feet (100 meters) there is no natural light at all. Fortunately many sea creatures are able to make their own light. In the same way that land animals use colors and patterns to identify one another, so the creatures of the deep use light.

Almost all squids can produce light. Types that live near the surface light up the undersides of their bodies to hide their shadows from predators swimming below. Other species dazzle their prey with bright searchlights in their tentacles. The deep-water squids also use light for communication. In rare glimpses we have from deep-sea exploration, we see them signalling to each other like little spaceships—flashing their lights on and off at will.

If an enemy comes too close, the squid can switch off all of its lights and disappear.

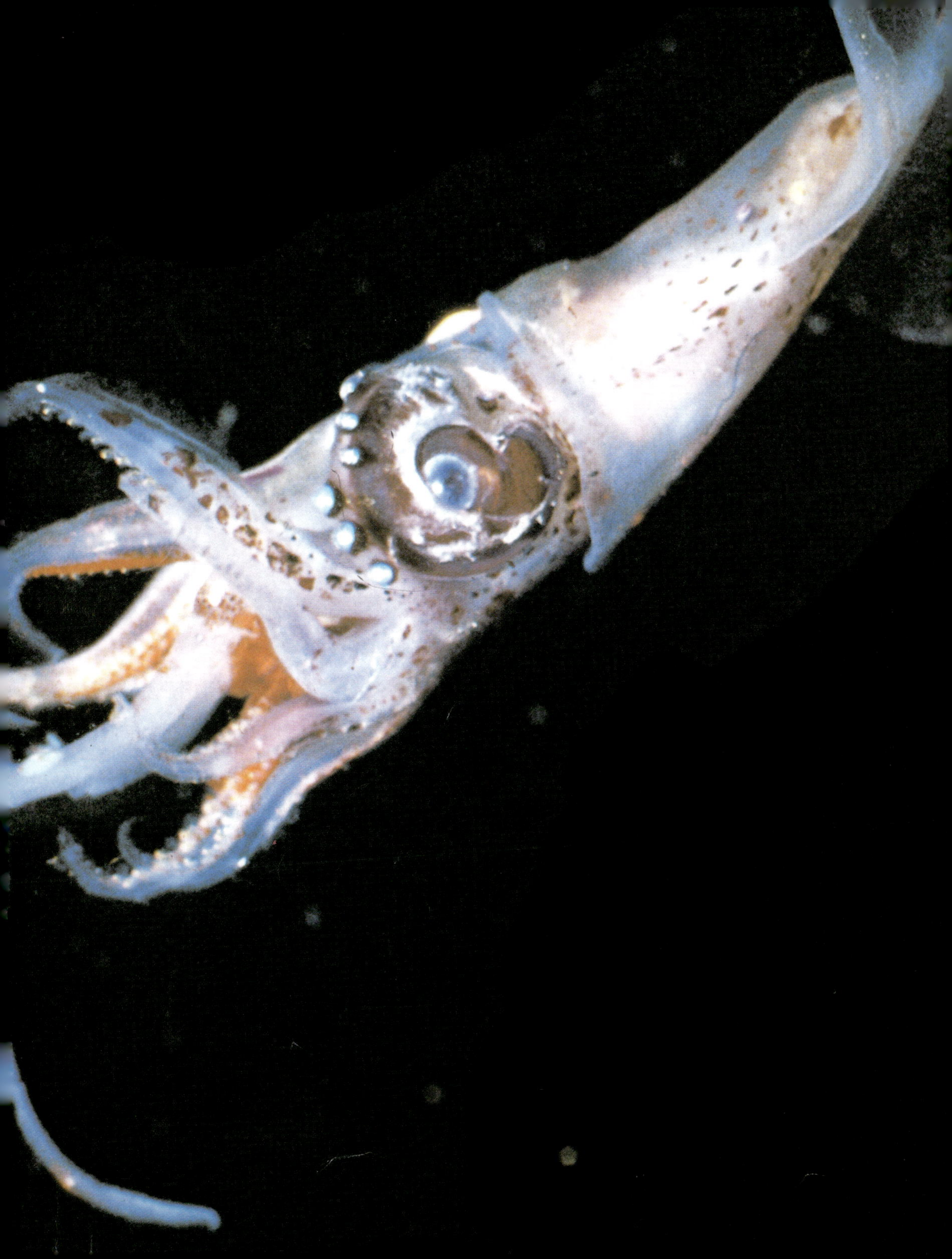

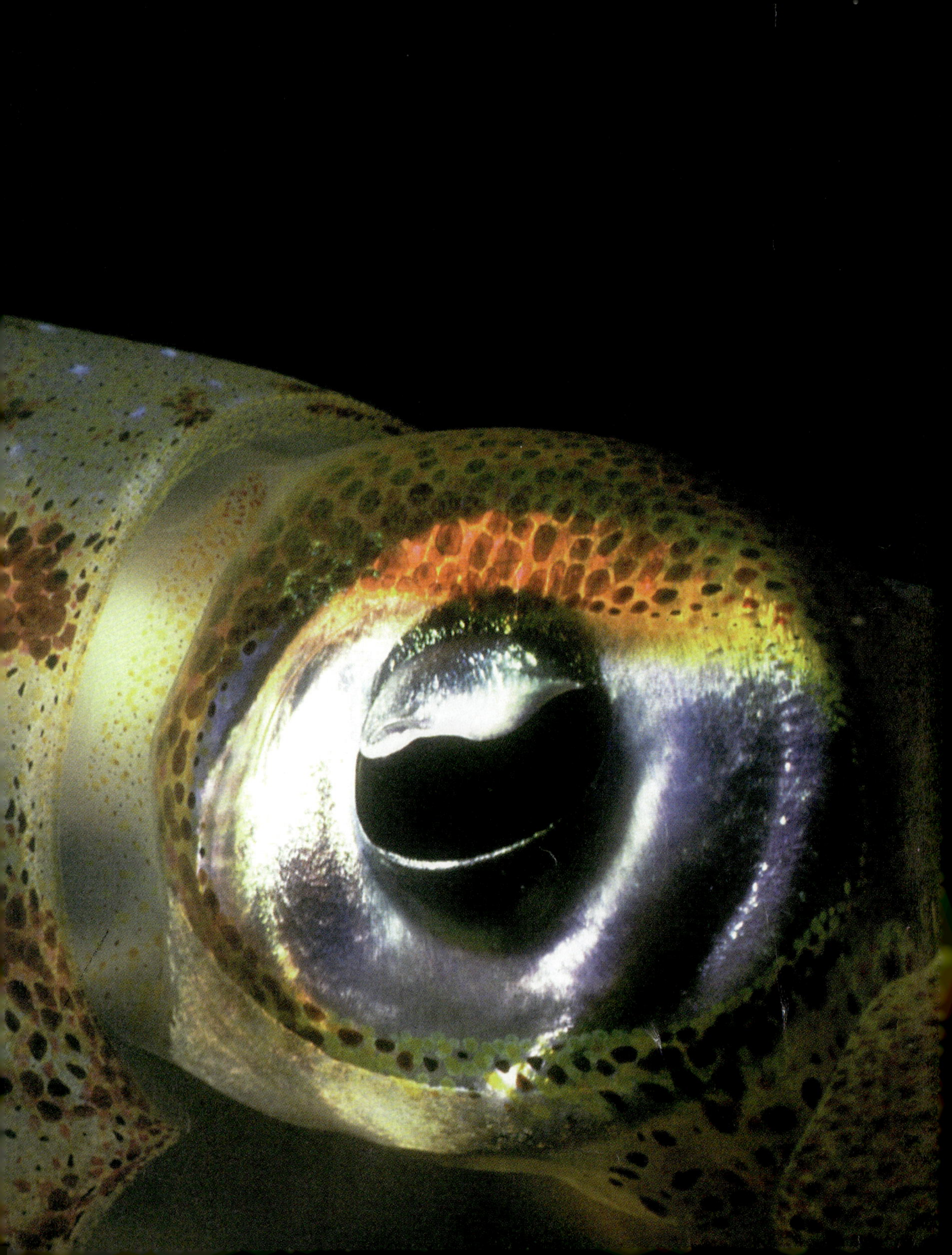

On the Lookout

Swimming through the ocean is hard work, and squids can't afford to waste energy. However, a squid has some remarkable senses that give it the best possible chance of finding food and staying out of the way of predators.

Like sharks, squids can taste tiny amounts of blood in the water using special pores in their skins. They may also be able to detect underwater sounds using delicate hairs on the outside of their bodies.

To help them to see through the dark and often murky seawater, squids have amazing eyesight. Our eyes are very similar in design to a squid's eyes. In some ways theirs are better—squids can look in front and behind at the same time. In relation to their size squids have the largest eyes of any animal. The eyes of a six-inch-long (15-centimeter) deep-sea squid could be the same size as yours!

Squids are always looking for their next meal.

Smart Creatures

For many animals a squid is the best snack in the ocean. With so many hungry eyes on the lookout, squids have to be smart to survive. Squids are famous for their quick thinking. They have the fastest reactions of any living creature. They also have much larger brains than any fish. Some scientists think that squids may be almost as intelligent as birds.

Octopuses are known to perform well in intelligence tests. They can open containers to get food, and even learn from one another. Because squids are so hard to keep in captivity, we do not really know how smart they are, but scientists think that they are at least as clever as octopuses.

A squid seizes a fish with its long tentacles. These attacks are so fast that, if the squid is on target, the prey has little chance of escape.

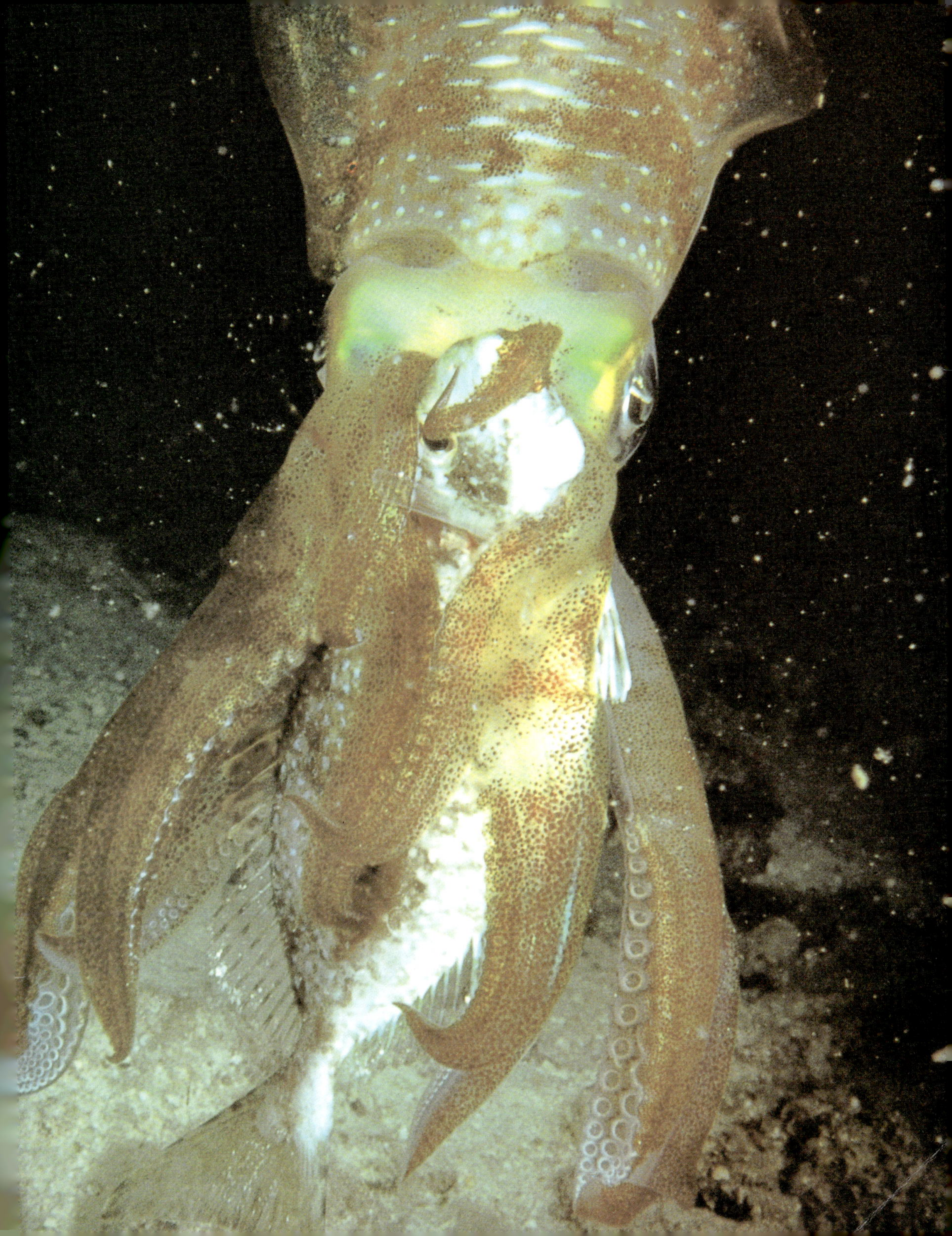

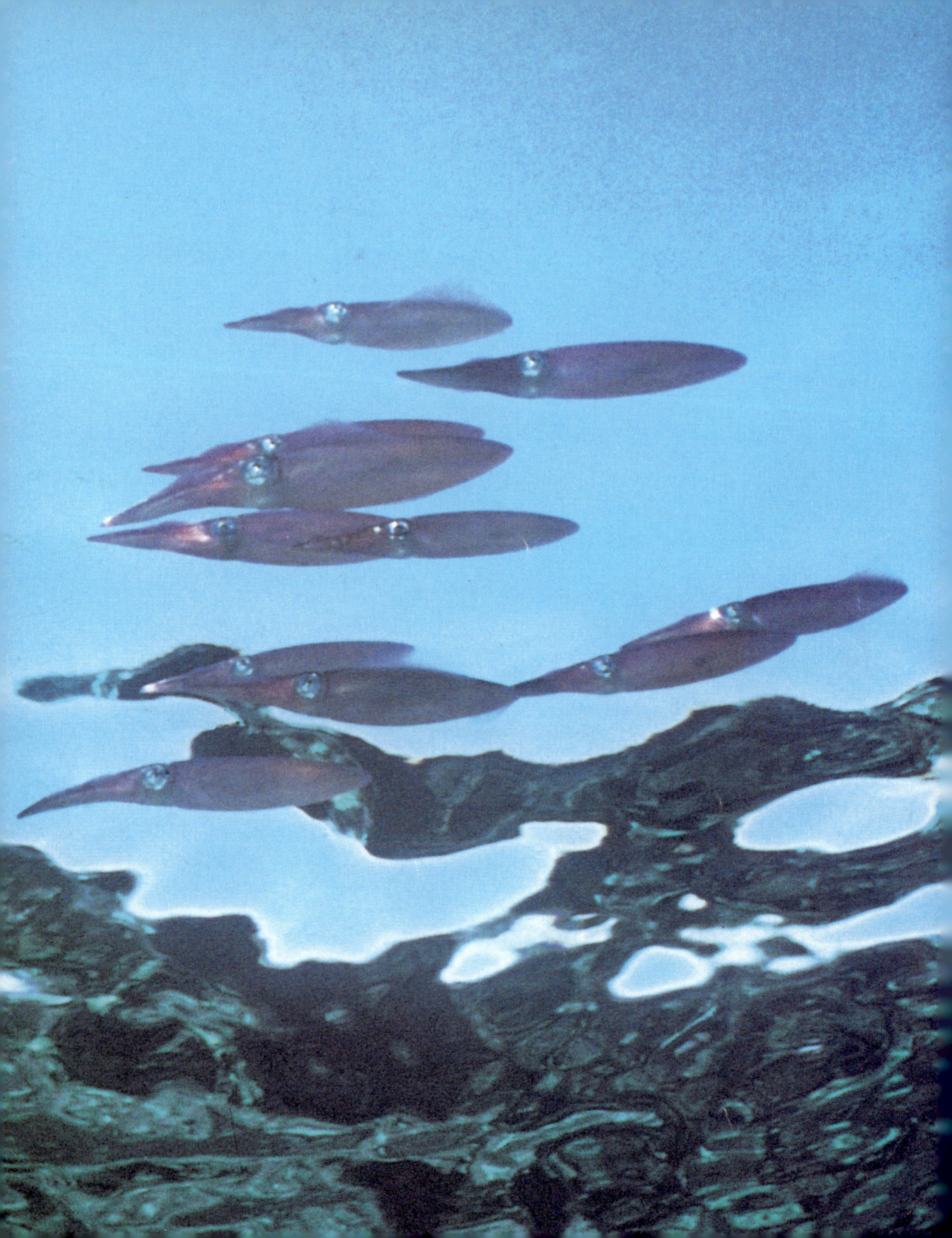

Life at the Surface

Most of the animal life in the oceans lives at or near to the surface. The water here is rich in oxygen, and plentiful sunlight allows plankton—a mixture of tiny plants and animals—to flourish. From tiny fish to giant whales, a wide variety of animals live here and feed on the plankton. Squids, too, inhabit these waters.

If you have ever seen or eaten a squid, it was probably caught near the surface. The long-finned and short-finned squids from the East Coast of the United States and the market squid from the West Coast are all common surface species known to be good eating. They have sleek, muscular bodies and live in large groups that we call schools. A school of squids has many pairs of eyes looking out for danger. If they are attacked, the squids scatter in all directions, confusing the predator.

Changing color to blend in, squids can be very hard to spot against the ocean surface.

Fierce Hunters

All squids are ferocious hunters. They will eat almost any animal that is small enough to catch, even other squids. In fact, large squids often shadow schools of their smaller relatives, catching and eating stragglers.

The most dangerous of all squids is the Humbolt squid, which lives off the west coast of South America. Local fishermen, who have seen these squids attacking large sharks and tunas, fear them so much that they will never get into the water when the squids are around. Against the fishermen's advice, one diver tried to film Humbolt squids hunting near the fishing boats at night. Within minutes of entering the water he was attacked. A tentacle wrapped around his neck, its sharp suckers cutting his skin. Another ripped the dive light from his hand. Panicking as the squid pulled him deeper into the water, he struggled free and made it back to the boat.

Streamlined and powerful, the Humbolt squid can grow to 12 feet (four meters) long.

31

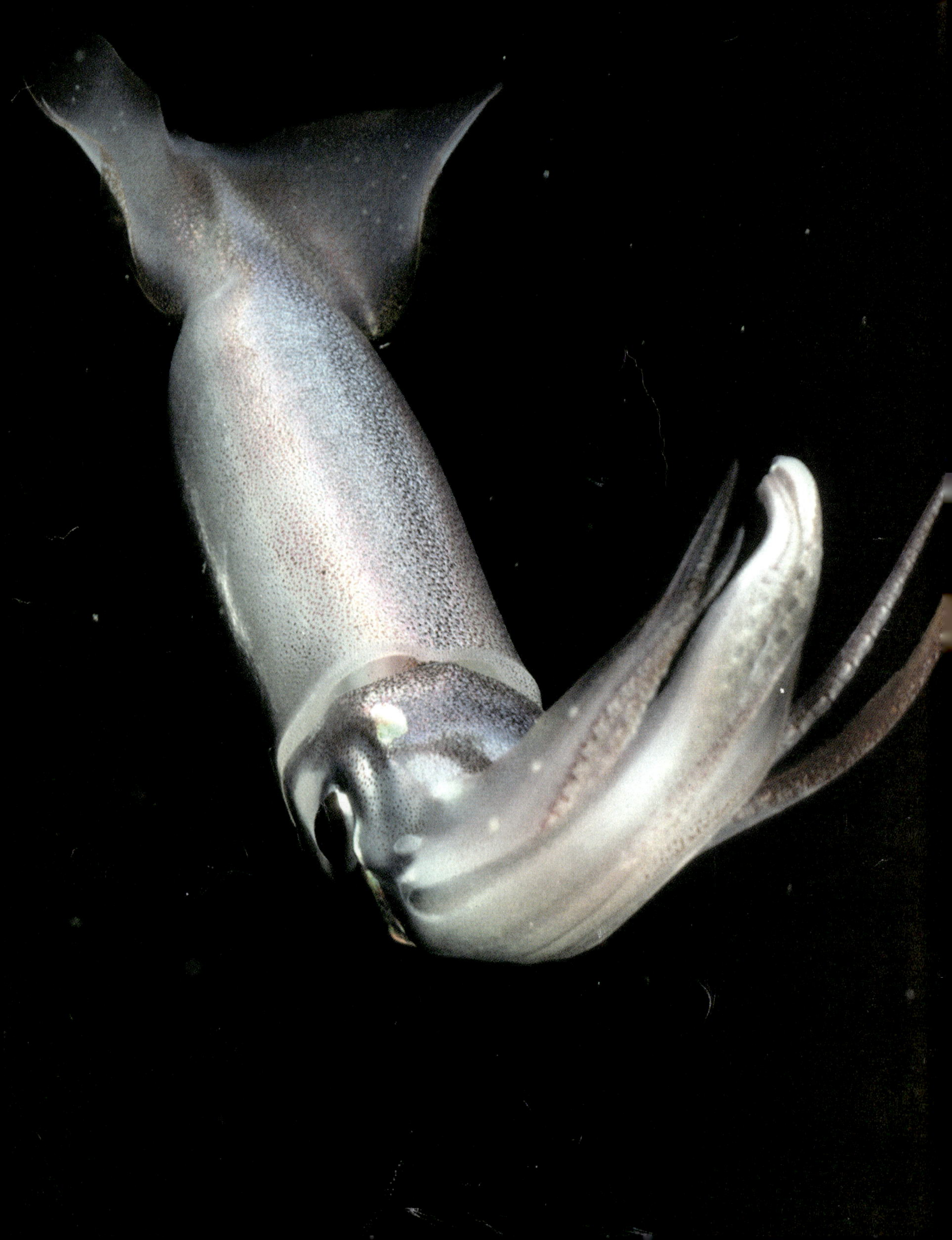

Getting Away

While squids terrorize anything smaller than they are, there are many large animals, such as sharks, dolphins, and tunas, that are always looking for a squid dinner! A squid, however, can be very hard to catch. First, using its fast reactions, the squid neatly sidesteps its opponent. Then it jets off at top speed, making sharp turns to confuse the hunter.

As a last resort a squid can squirt out a thick cloud of ink that hangs in the water behind it. The squid then turns see-through and swims away, leaving the confused predator with a mouthful of ink!

Some of the fastest squids will even jump into the air to avoid enemies. By squirting water out of their funnels, they can fly across the surface for up to 45 feet (15 meters), landing safely away from the danger.

Using their arms and fins, squids can make sharp turns as they swim.

Deep-Water Dwellers

Over three-quarters of the ocean floor, an area larger that all the dry land put together, is more than one mile (1,600 meters) below the surface. The animals that live here spend all their lives in complete darkness and in water that is very cold. Without sunlight no plants can grow, but a gentle "snow," made up of the bodies of surface plants and animals, falls from above, feeding the deep-sea creatures.

The first explorers to peer into this unknown world through the windows of deep-diving submarines were amazed by what they saw. Most had expected few animals to survive in such harsh conditions, but a host of fish, sharks, and squids were drawn toward the submarines' bright lights.

Although they are known only from these rare sightings, squids are probably common in the deep ocean. We know almost nothing about their lifestyles, numbers, or sizes. Imagine the monsters that could be lurking in the darkness beyond our searchlights.

Unlike surface types, most deep-water squids have delicate, gel-like bodies. Usually they are seen alone, drifting through the water and grabbing any small fish or squids that come within reach.

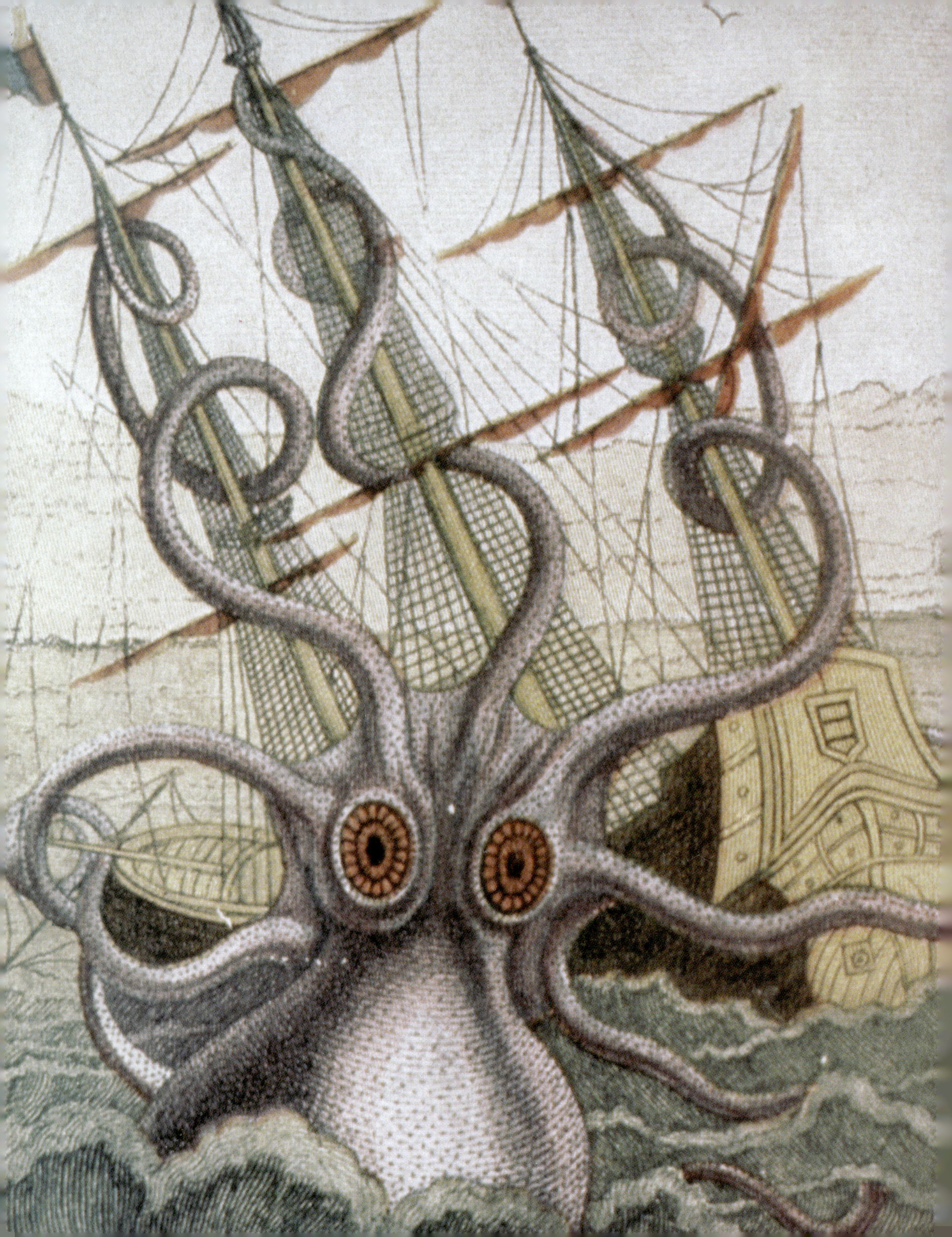

The Kraken

Hundreds of years ago sailors from Norway told stories of a many-armed monster that pulled whole ships under the water and ate their crews. The terrible creature, called the Kraken, became the most famous of all sea-monsters. Most people, however, thought that Krakens, like mermaids and sea-serpents, were imaginary creatures, not real animals.

In October 1873, off Portugal Cove in Canada, two fishermen were investigating what they thought was a large piece of wreckage floating in the bay. As their small boat drew near, the floating shape opened out like a gigantic umbrella revealing two huge green eyes. The fishermen froze in terror—they had disturbed a Kraken! The monstrous creature immediately launched its attack, wrapping a long tentacle around the boat. Bravely, one of the men cut through the tentacle with a small axe. The injured Kraken disappeared, leaving the shaken fishermen to return home, carrying its tentacle.

Opposite page:
A large ship falls victim to the Kraken in this 19th-century painting.

Sea-Monster Sightings

The tentacle was sold to a local naturalist who identified it as belonging to a squid. However, at 18 feet (six meters) long, the tentacle must have belonged to a squid far larger than any known at that time. Clearly the Kraken was not make-believe, it was a giant squid.

Since this first sighting the bodies of many giant squids have been found on beaches all around the world. The largest ever recorded washed up at Thimble Tickle Bay in Canada. It was 55 feet (17 meters) long and weighed more than 2,000 pounds (900 kilograms)—10 times the weight of a full-grown man. Like most stranded squids, it was a female. Males are smaller and seem to be extremely rare.

The giant squid is a terrifying creature that may be responsible for many of our sea-monster stories, but what do we actually know about this rarely seen animal?

Giant Squid Facts

Unfortunately for scientists, but luckily for the rest of us, humans do not meet giant squids very often. All that we know about them comes from sightings of dead or dying animals washed up on beaches. No one has ever seen a healthy one. A dead giant squid's body is brick red. When alive, however, they can probably change color. Giant squids have the largest eyes of any animal, the size of volleyballs. Adults live in deep, cold water and feed mainly on fish, sharks, and other squids. Male sperm whales are probably the only animals large enough to hunt full-grown giant squids.

The giant squid has a large brain and may be very intelligent, which could explain why it has been so successful at avoiding people. If we went out to capture a giant squid today, we still wouldn't know where to start looking.

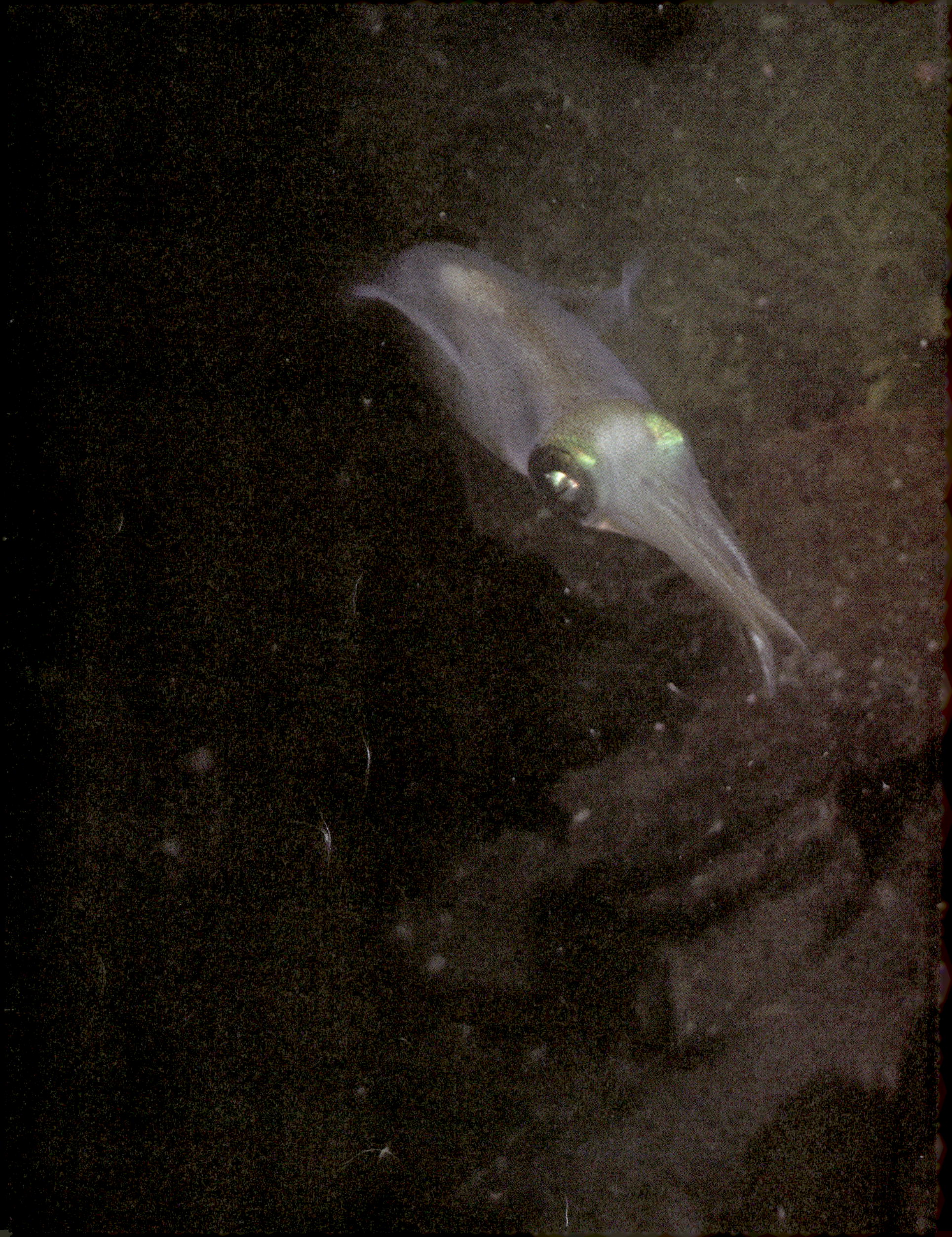

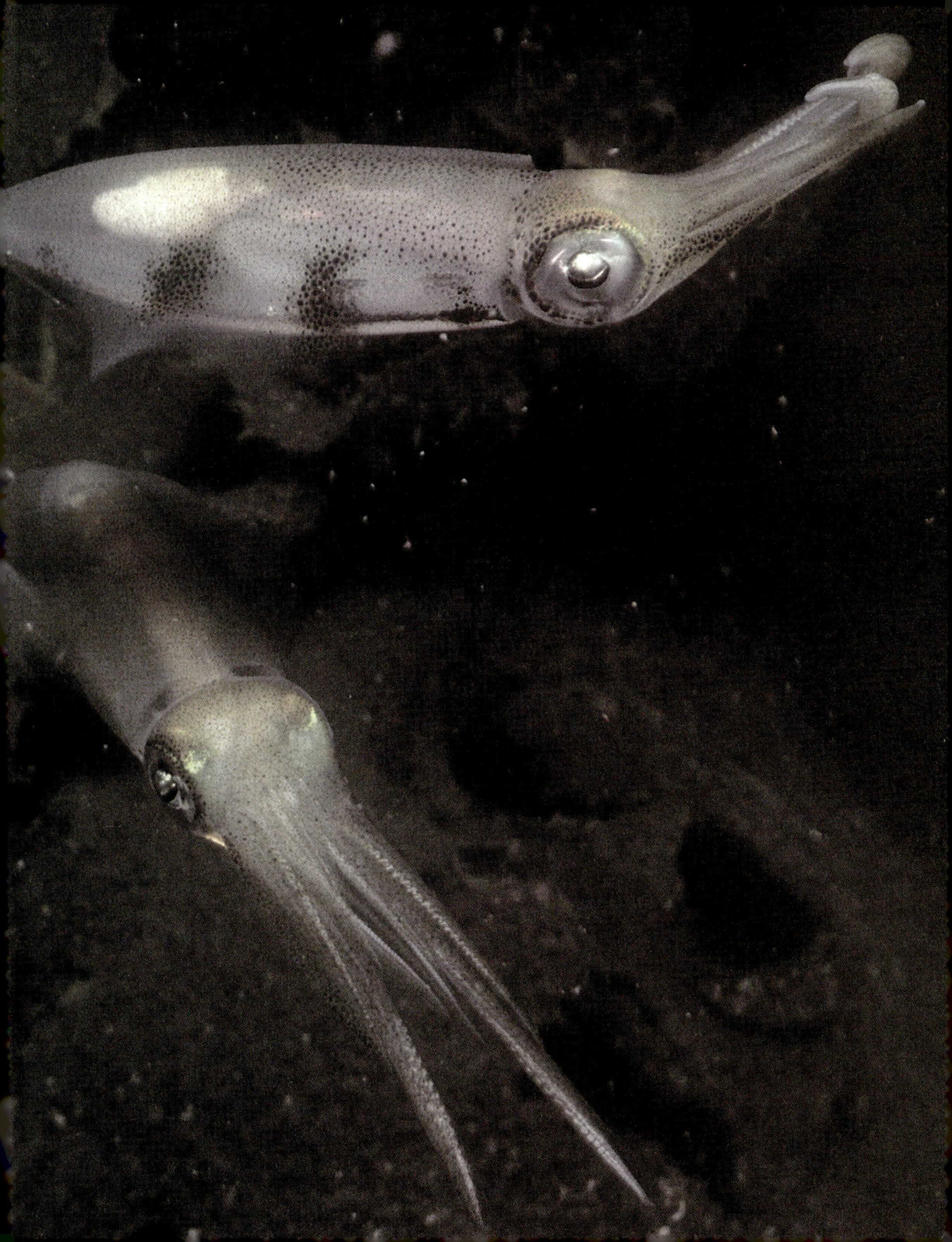

The Next Generation

While we can only imagine how giant squids produce their young, the common surface types come together in vast schools to breed. The squids in these schools are often so tightly packed that they look like a solid mass, and this is the only time that they become easy to catch. Fishermen follow the schools and fill their nets, but with so many squids there are always plenty left to lay eggs.

The squids in the school pair up, each male swims below his mate flashing bright colors across his body. Then he reaches into her mantle using one of his arms and fertilizes her eggs. The sticky eggs are laid together in large masses that are attached to rocks or left to float freely in the open ocean.

Squids mate only once in their lives. The exhausted adults die a few days after the eggs have been laid.

A female squid rests on a mass of eggs.

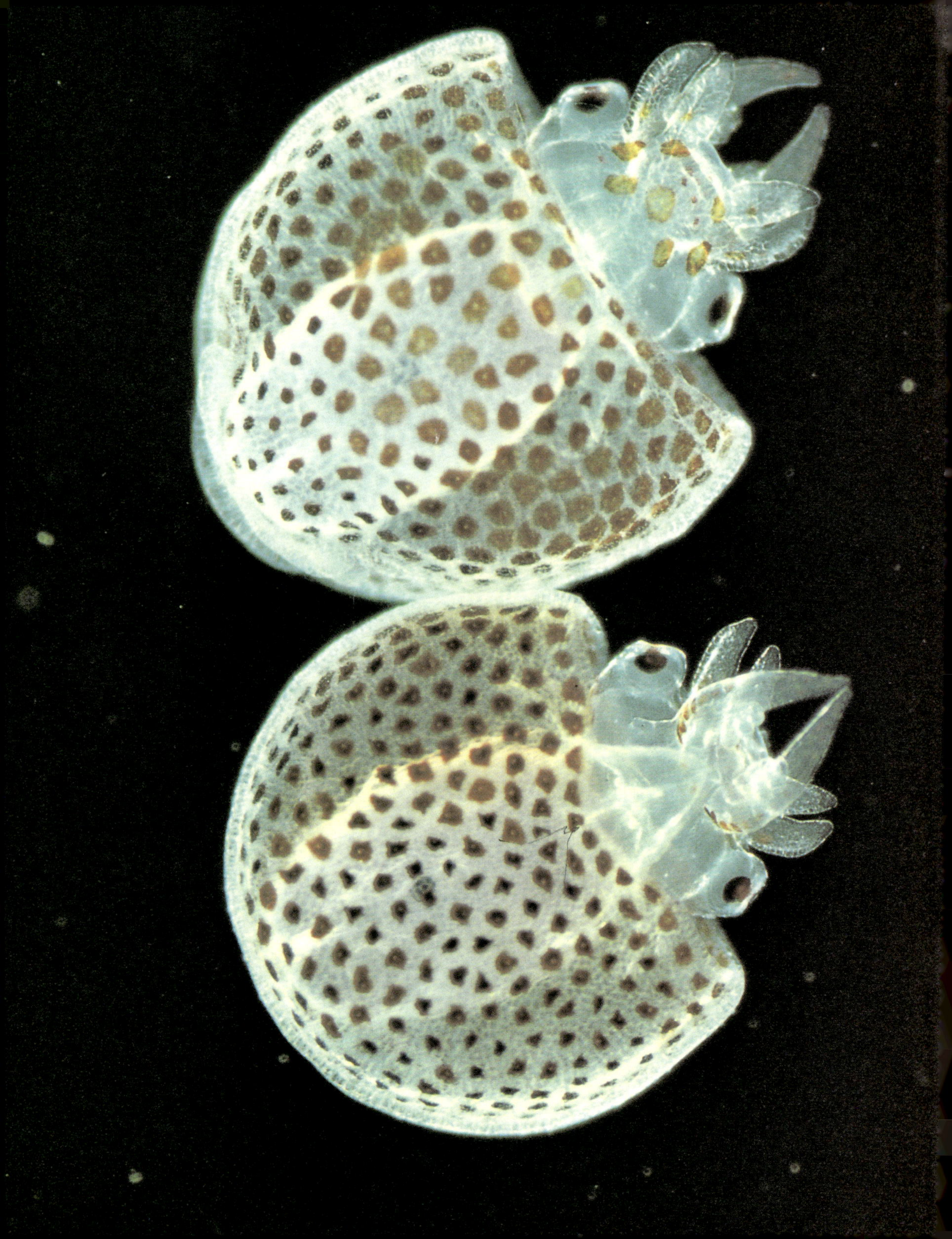

Living Fast, Dying Young

The young squids develop quickly inside their eggs. Squid eggs have a taste that is unpleasant to most animals, so a large proportion hatch safely. The baby squid looks like a miniature version of its parents and joins millions of other tiny animals in the plankton. Already it has all the skills it needs to catch the tiny fish and shrimps on which it feeds. This is a dangerous time, however, as many young squids are caught and eaten by predators. The lucky few that survive grow large enough to leave the plankton and form schools of their own. Many squids live out their whole lives in less than a year.

This way of life sounds wasteful. Fish often live for much longer than squids and breed many times in their lives. Squids, however, by living dangerously and dedicating all of their efforts to breeding just once, can lay enough eggs to guarantee that there will be a new generation next year.

Opposite page: *Living in the plankton is very dangerous, so baby squids must grow fast.*

Unknown Animals

Squids are among the most successful and important animals in the oceans. Each year sperm whales alone are estimated to eat 100 million tons of squids, yet this does not even seem to dent their numbers. If we could figure out how to catch them efficiently, they could be a very useful source of food for people, too.

Today increasing pollution and global warming are changing our oceans in ways we cannot predict. Squids are very vulnerable to pollution, and many types cannot survive in water only a few degrees warmer than normal. Our futures and the futures of squids depend on how we choose to treat our environment. If we make the wrong choices, we run the risk of destroying these fascinating animals before we have begun to learn their secrets.

Words to Know

Arms Limbs used mainly for holding onto objects. Squids have eight arms.

Chameleon A type of lizard able to change its color to match its surroundings.

Funnel The flexible tube underneath a squid's head.

Global warming The gradual warming of the earth due to harmful gases being released into the air.

Ink A colored liquid. Most squids squirt out blue-black ink when threatened.

Mantle The muscular sac at the rear of a squid's body.

Oxygen A gas that is found in air and dissolved in water. All animals need to breathe oxygen to stay alive.

Plankton A mixture of tiny animals and plants living close to the surface of the ocean.

Predator An animal that hunts other animals for food.

Prey An animal that is hunted by other animals.

Streamlined Smooth and sleek, able to move through water or air easily.

Tentacles The two long limbs that a squid can shoot out to capture its prey.

INDEX

arms, 6, 13, 17, 33, 42, 47

beak, 6, 13, 17
blue-ringed octopus, 12; *illus.*, 12
breeding, 42

camouflage, 21, 29
cephalopod, 12, 13
color, 21, 29, 39, 42, 47
cuttlefish, 13

deep-water squids, 22, 34, 35;
 illus., 35
defense, 18, 21, 22, 29, 33, 45
diet, 17, 30, 34, 35, 39, 45

eggs, 42; *illus.*, 43
eyes, 25, 29, 39

fins, 6, 17, 33
funnel, 14, 15, 47

giant squids, 37, 38, 39

Humbolt squid, 18, 30, 31;
 illus., 19, 31
hunting, 13, 17, 22, 26, 31

ink, 21, 33, 47
intelligence, 26, 39

Kraken, the, 37; *illus.*, 36

light production, 22

mantle, 6, 14, 42
mollusks, 9, 10

nautilus, 10; *illus.*, 11

octopus, 9, 12, 13, 26

pen, 6, 10, 13
plankton, 29, 45, 47
popeye squid, 17; *illus.*, 16
predators, 18, 22, 25, 26, 29, 33, 42, 45, 47. *See* sperm whale
prey, 17, 18, 22, 26, 35, 47

schools, 29, 42
senses, 17, 25
snails, 9, 10; *illus.*, 8
sperm whale, 18, 39, 46
suckers, 6, 10, 18, 30
swimming, 6, 14, 15, 25, 33

tentacles, 6, 10, 17, 18, 22, 26, 30, 37, 38, 47

young squid, 45; *illus.*, 44

Cover Photo: Jeffrey L. Rotman / Corbis
Photo Credits: Stephen Frink / Corbis, pages 4, 15, 24; Jeffrey L. Rotman / Corbis, pages 7, 32, 40; Laurie Campbell / NHPA, page 8; Dr. Eckart Pott / NHPA, page 11; ANT Photo Library / NHPA, page 12; Stuart Westmorland / Corbis, page 16; Norbert Wu / NHPA, pages 19, 20, 28, 31, 43; Agence Nature / NHPA, page 23; Bill Wood / NHPA, page 27; Bruce Robison / Corbis, page 35; Corbis-Bettmann, page 36; Peter Parks / NHPA, page 44.

DATE DUE			

High Meadows School
Library Media Center
1055 Willeo Road
Roswell, GA 30075